This book is dedicated to my wonderful husband who has supported my dreams selflessly – I could never thank you enough!

# MANAGING and CONDITIONING
# THE EVENT HORSE

Preparing your horse for Horse Trials through the Advanced Level.

**ELIZABETH GRISELL-SHORT**

ISBN# 978-0-578-01104-2

# TABLE OF CONTENTS

# PREFACE

In writing this book I have made every effort to provide accurate information and good advice. However, every horse is an individual, and different climates require variations of management techniques. I want to make it very clear that I am offering a book of guidelines only. I had this book reviewed by many top-level event riders, vets, farriers and equine nutrition experts. I took all of their advice into consideration in developing this book. Neither the publisher nor the author assumes any responsibility for the results of following the guidelines in this book. Each person is responsible for their own decisions in the management of their horses. Each horse must be evaluated on an individual basis. Manufacturers of any products mentioned in this book are also not responsible for results obtained from the use of such products.

# EVENTING VS. HORSE TRIALS

Eventing is a three-part competition consisting of dressage, cross-country and stadium jumping. Dressage is where the horse is asked to carry out a precise pattern of movements in a balanced, rhythmical manner to test his obedience and suppleness. This is the only phase that is subjectively judged. Cross-country jumping tests the horse's jumping, endurance and speed abilities. The horse is timed and faulted for being too fast or too slow on the course, as well as jumping faults. The stadium jumping phase tests stamina and accuracy, jumping a course of colorful jumps. Here the horses are faulted for speed requirements as well as clearing the jumps.

Eventing has its roots as a comprehensive cavalry test requiring mastery of several types of riding. It has two main formats, the one day event (1DE), and the three day event (3DE). This book deals with conditioning for the One or Two Day Events; also called Horse Trials. Horse Trials can be training and conditioning for a Three Day Event. Most people competing in the sport of "Eventing" are competing in Horse Trials. The Olympic level of eventing is the four star event (CCI****), a Three Day Event at the Advanced Level.

The event horse is required to be an athelete in every way. He must be very fit and very disciplined. At the upper levels he must be in peak condition to be successful in competition. It takes years of progressive conditioning to attain the peak cardiovascular and musculo-skeletal capacity required for success and soundness in the upper levels. Every aspect of the horse's life must support his effort. His nutrition requirements become more complicated as he advances up the levels of competition. Conditioning also becomes more complex, as he falls between speed horses and endurance horses. The event horse must be conditioned to compete in jumping (an anaerobic discipline) as well as dressage (an aerobic discipline). The cross-country phase includes aerobic and anaerobic exercise. The program in this book includes nutrition, progressive conditioning schedules and suggestions to keep the event horse sound and successful!

This book started as a manual for my students. It has been written as a book for the management of competing sport horses, specifically in eventing. There are many books on the market that teach the sport of eventing: the types of horses to buy, the different phases of the sport, equipment needed, rules that apply in competition, riding the courses or dressage tests, etc. There is a need for these books, and I suggest you read as many of them as you can. This book provides examples of conditioning schedules to follow for eventing horses. It provides guidelines for the proper management of horses as athletes, stable management and conditioning management. You will find answers to questions like: what to feed sport horses, and how to prepare them physically and mentally for their level of competition.

**It is very unfair for a rider to ask a horse to compete in this sport without proper conditioning.** Most horses will enjoy eventing as much as we do if they are properly prepared. I have seen so many people show up at events with horses that are obviously unfit and unprepared for what they are asked to do. Bless these horses' hearts, they give all they have and go home without the riders ever realizing how sore they may be the next day. For your horses' sake, learn all you can about preparing them for the rigors of this demanding sport. Gain knowledge from every source possible, then use what works best for you and each horse you condition.

I have spent years developing these guidelines, changing them as I learned more about these magnificent, athletic horses and this challenging sport. I have studied equine management, nutrition, conditioning, and combined training from many different sources including: instructors, clinics, books, videotapes, university classes, and veterinary seminars.

Become a student and learn everything you can about what your horses need in order to perform their best and stay in peak condition. Do your research and study other books on nutrition, conditioning, dressage, and jumping as well. You will find a helpful list in the appendices. My horses are all on a management program based on this book, but all have individual needs that differ from each other. **I am in no way offering a rigid schedule, but rather a place to start and customize to your needs!** For example, thoroughbreds are much easier to condition than most any other breed. The athletic ability, breeding and temperament of your horse will determine the type of conditioning and schedule you will need to follow. **It is important to realize that horses are individuals and require individual care; I cannot stress this enough.**

# THE RIDER

Let me tell you one big secret of great riders: they ride all the time as if they don't have stirrups!! This will give you a strong seat, tight legs, better balance, the ability to have soft hands, and also save your horse's back. An event rider must be in excellent physical condition, mostly due to the demands of the cross-country course. On the cross-country course the horse is cantering or galloping up to several miles. During this time you must be able to hold yourself up off the saddle in a balanced galloping position using only your legs. While your muscles are requiring more oxygen to work so hard, your brain is giving some up. This alone can result in a lack of judgment during the most dangerous phase of eventing. Adopt a fitness program for yourself and make sure you are not overweight!! Join the USEA (United States Eventing Association) in addition to your local eventing and dressage associations to learn all you can. Audit many clinics pertaining to jumping, dressage, eventing, etc. Try to take your horse to the clinics if you can afford the time and expense.

Tack and saddle fitting are very important to keep your horse from becoming sore. Locate a good saddlery that can help you properly reflock or fit your saddle to your horse. The saddle you purchase is likely to be narrow, medium or a wide tree. But the saddle fitting doesn't end there. The saddler can then flock the saddle to fit your individual horse's back and withers exactly. The saddler can also check your bridle and other tack for correct fit.

An important skill to master in eventing is the ability to judge your speed on your horse. Speed in eventing is measured metrically. An average walking horse is moving at 125 meters per minute. The average trot is 250 m/min, with a strong trot about 300 m/min. A canter averages 350 m/min. while a gallop is approximately 500 m/min. Obviously these depend on the individual horse, but you must learn to gain an idea of how fast you are going at any given time. One of the best way to do this is to set up a few markers at different lengths, and time yourself on your horse to determine how fast he is traveling. You could set up a certain color of flags every 100 meters. Then walk from one flag to the next and determine the time it took. Another color could be used to determine the speed of your horse at different trots. Other colors could be used at 350 meters and 500 meters. A stopwatch will be necessary for this exercise. You will then have a much better idea on the cross-country course of your horse's speed. You will need to know what your time should be in the middle of your cross-country ride and where that midpoint is on the course. A metric measuring wheel is well worth your investment to determine your distances on the cross-country courses.

If you come across a word or phrase in this book that you are do not know or understand, please look it up in a related book and educate yourself about it. Riders need an instructor and vet who can teach them special care techniques. They need to learn how to gallop a horse, how to know their speed, how to ride different fences, how to ride different exercises, how to bandage the horse for different needs. Find trainers, vets, farriers and clinics for these educational purposes. Do not pay attention to fads in the horse world. Ask your veterinarian about your management decisions and pay the most attention to your horse's health. I have provided a list of informative books and videos on various topics in the back of this book. You are responsible for your own education. Read and learn everything you can on these topics and then use common sense in putting together a management and conditioning program for your horse.

# NUTRITION MANAGEMENT

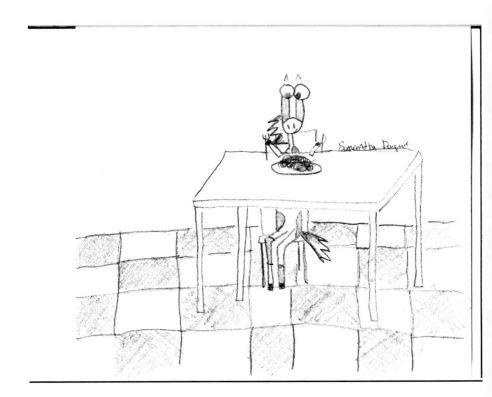

My philosophy of management throughout my program remains the same: "Horses are meant to be horses, outside grazing and moving - that is what they are built for, physically and psychologically."

First of all, let's look at your horse's nutrition. Your nutrition program should be designed for a hard working horse that is developing muscles and strengthening his skeletal system. Your pasture, hay, and feed, need to work together to achieve this goal. The amount of each type of feed depends on the horse.

# HAY MANAGEMENT

The amount of calcium should be twice the amount of phosphorous in the horse's diet. It is important to note that alfalfa and grass hay can be offered together to balance the ratios of calcium and phosphorus. Grass hays are higher in phosphorous and lower in calcium than recommended ratios. Alfalfa hay is higher in calcium and lower in phosphorous than recommended amounts. The two together in equal amounts will balance each other out.

Some people don't like feeding alfalfa hay. This is fine as long as you offer a mineral supplement that is higher in calcium and magnesium, while containing lower amounts of phosphorous to help balance out the two. Grains and grasses are both higher in phosphorous. Not enough calcium can cause weak bone strength and muscle problems. In places like California where people feed lots of alfalfa, you need to be careful because too much calcium can cause enteroliths in the horse's intestines, as well as other problems. Enteroliths are stones that build up over time and can cause a blockage.

Make sure to buy your hay from a grower that tests the soil and fertilizes it annually to keep it high in nutrients. **Know the selenium content of your feed, grass and hays!** Be sure you are feeding enough, but not too much selenium. The concentration of a daily ration should be .1 ppm of selenium. Always have your grain, hay and grass tested to be sure you are feeding the proper balance of minerals. Testing is usually a free service offered by a state agricultural department.

The type of grass hay available will differ from area to area. The decision of what type of grass hay you should use will depend on the grass your horses are eating in their paddocks. Buy hay that will complement your grass, not comprised of the same type of grass. This practice will offer the horse a variety of grasses in his diet, ultimately giving him a variety of nutrients. Choose high quality grass hay known for absorbing nutrients from the soil. For example, in the southeast a native grass is fescue, but it is not a high quality grass because it fails to pick up nutrients from the soil. You could also feed high quality alfalfa hay as well, to balance the grass hay.

Alfalfa can be purchased as a hay, cube or pellet. Most farms will have grass growing in the horse's pasture in the summer, but not in the winter. In the winter, feed grass hay along with alfalfa. In the summer, if your horse is eating grass in his paddocks, a flake or two of alfalfa will complement it. However, a horse standing in a stall must be offered a balanced mix of hay to keep his gut moving.

# PASTURE MANAGEMENT

Keeping horses is also a type of farming. You will need to "farm" your grass to offer healthy grazing for your horse. You should plant grass in your paddocks or pastures. Two acres per horse should be sufficient to prevent pastures from becoming "horse-poor." If your pastures are not in need of mowing every month, they may be horse-poor.

Pastures need to be picked out once a week and harrowed once a month. Harrowing is not recommended in the winter for most areas because there aren't enough insects to break down the manure.

Make sure your pasture is growing healthy grass. Annual soil tests and proper application of fertilizers, lime, etc. will help to keep the grass healthier. Most grazing grasses are healthiest for the horses between four inches and eight inches. Less than four inches the grass is still immature and can contain extra carbohydrates. Once the grass exceeds eight inches most varieties will start to produce seeds, decreasing the nutrient value. To keep the pastures healthy, allow the grass to grow to eight inches before cutting it back to four inches. Take a soil sample annually and fertilize accordingly. This will increase the amount of nutrients available to the grass, and therefore to your horse. If you are opposed to fertilizing, you could still test the soil and correct the pH balance with natural lime. This would allow minerals to release from the soil and be available for the grass to pick up.

When the grass is kept healthy it can outgrow the weeds. Mowing will help keep weeds from maturing and multiplying. Remember that horses eat grasses, but not many weeds. You may need to mow often to manage the weeds. Resting and rotating pastures is also necessary to keep them healthy.

CAUTION: if you fertilize a pasture, rest the area afterward to avoid causing the horses to develop laminitis. A good rule of thumb to follow is to mow the pasture low before you fertilize and then to avoid grazing a horse on it until it has been mowed again. Fertilizer causes the grass to store excess carbohydrates, a leading cause of founder in horses.

Horses in training should be turned out in individual lots with shelters. This prevents many injuries occurring from horses playing hard together.

My horses are in two-acre lots next to each other. They still socialize with each other and play along the fence line together. Most of them have a horse on either side and they all can see the barn and what is going on around the farm. Individual turn out will also help in the control of pests and parasites.

# SETTING UP HORSE KEEPING

It is optimal to have the horse on pasture at least twelve hours a day, but if he grows fat on this quantity of grazing you may be forced to restrict him to a "dry lot" for part of this time. It is vital that he is still in an area of unrestricted movement and may roam freely. I have to caution the use of a dry lot in sandy areas where sand colic may result. Sand colic should be prevented with a weeklong monthly treatment of fiber therapy, or a vet recommended schedule.

The remaining twelve hours of your horse's day could be in his stall, which is preferably attached to a small lot, allowing him to walk in or out at will. In other words, twelve hours is too long for a horse to stand in a stall without being able to move freely. Putting a horse in a stall is the equivalent to keeping a dog in a crate. It is necessary and useful, but should not be done for long periods of time; that is unfair to the animal. Breaking up a horse's stall time in this manner will go a long way to prevent stable vices and other psychological problems. Horses who are allowed to move freely on their own twenty-four hours a day have fewer problems with tearing ligaments and tendons when they are in work. This makes sense because they keep their legs warmed up by moving freely.

Colic is currently the number one cause of death in horses. For the most part, horses will never colic if they are on full time pasture and a good worming program. We should alter their natural environment as little as possible. It is ideal to have horses turned out on quality pasture in the daytime during winter and at night during the summer. Heat is hard on horses and a fan in the summer is great relief from heat and flies. A fan could be placed in an in-and-out stall, or in the horse's shelter. It is amazing how fast your horse will learn to stand in front of the fan to stay cool and keep away flies!! Be sure to keep the electric cords out of reach of the horse's mouth; chewing on a cord could kill your horse.

# FEEDING GRAIN

Horses need forage to be the bulk of their total food intake because their intestines are free flowing inside them. They are not anchored in place with connective tissue like human intestines. This is why horses can end up with a twist in their gut. If you picture the horse's intestines to be like an empty sausage skin (or tube), you can see how part of the "tube" could be full while the empty sections would be collapsible. This allows them to fold in on themselves, then allowing the full section to flip over itself, twisting the gut. This is why it is so important for horses to have forage constantly moving through them at a slow rate. The action of the horse moving is what helps keep his intestines moving and pushing food along through the tube. This is another reason horses need to have freedom of movement.

Grain, or the commercial feed we buy in bags to supplement our horse's diet, is much heavier than the hay or grass a horse slowly eats. Grain is not natural for a horse to eat. It requires an increase in the amount of acid pumped into the horse's stomach for digestion. Because the grain then creates a heavy spot in the intestines as it is moved through, it also sets the scene for colic or a twisted gut. The best feeds are light in weight, easy to digest and are only used to supplement the horse's forage diet. Grain also contains less fiber, impacting in the horse's gut and leading to colic. A horse's stomach cannot contain more than five pounds of grain. The best way to feed grain is to offer small amounts at a time, never exceeding two pounds at a time. A horse receiving more than a total of five pounds of grain a day is five times more likely to colic than a horse receiving only grass and hay. Some barn managers break up the grain feedings up to four times a day to help prevent colic and ulcers. Ulcers are another common problem with horses kept in stalls, stressful situations, and heavy training.

The current thoughts on feeding grain are supportive of lower protein content for less active horses. But remember, we are feeding horses that are in medium to heavy training, therefore the recommended grain is in the range of 12-14 percent protein. Now before you protest this amount of protein in the grain, keep this in mind – if a horse is fed one pound of 14% protein feed in a day, and another horse is fed two pounds of 7% protein feed in a day, both those horses are getting the same amount of protein. The grain should be a supplement to high quality hay and pasture. Remember, don't feed very much grain (concentrate); the bulk of the diet should be quality hay or fresh grazing.

It is recommended that a horse on his day off has his feed ration cut back or in half, therefore helping to avoid "Monday Morning Syndrome," also known as "tying up" or "azoturia." Another way to accomplish this is to have a "work out" feed which the horse does not receive on his days off. You could use grain or a mash, adding extra electrolytes when the horse may need it due to excessive sweating.

Common sense is required in the amount of feed portioned to your animals. **A horse in training should not be overweight.** Extra weight will add stress to the horse's joints in dressage, jumping and galloping. This extra weight can be dangerous to a horse on the cross-country phase by making it hard for the horse to cool himself efficiently. It is just plain cruel to have a horse who is over weight in this sport. You are in complete control of how fit or fat your horse is. It is your responsibility to keep your horse sound, and keeping him fit is a big contributor. If your horse is an easy keeper, cut out his grain before cutting out his hay. Some horses can't have grain or alfalfa and will do fine on just grass hay with minerals to balance his calcium and phosphorous ratios. It is more important to keep the horse at a proper weight and mineral balance than to give him grain.

Beet pulp is a good feed to use for making a mash at shows or for workout feeds. It contains more calories than hay and is digested in the hindgut. The advantage of this is that large fluctuations of blood sugar are avoided. To feed beet pulp you will need to soak it in an equal amount of water for at least twelve hours before feeding, to properly hydrate it. You can mix some of the horse's grain into the mash to make it more appetizing. It is a very good idea to feed the mash everyday or every workout feed. Feeding the mash at shows can be beneficial in preventing the horse from developing colic or forming ulcers due to stress.

# WEIGHT MANAGEMENT

**Every horse is different. Some are hard keepers and some are easy keepers; you must know your horse. Ask your vet if you are not sure if your horse is on the thin or heavy side.** It can also be a good idea to ask other people how they see your horse, as you see him everyday it can be hard for you to determine if he has lost or gained weight. An overweight horse will have fat pads on either side of his tail and/or a cresty neck. A thin horse's ribs will be visible, and/or their hipbones. A general rule of thumb is that you should be able to feel the horse's ribs but not see them. Ask your vet to assess your horse's weight if you aren't sure of his condition. You can purchase a height/weight tape to track your horse's weight.

Another accurate way of determining the weight of your horse is to measure the circumference of your horse's heart girth (value A). Then measure the length of your horse's body, from his point of shoulder to his point of rump (value B). Heart girth x heart girth x body length divided by 300 plus 50 equals the weight. AxAxB/300+50=weight.

The event horses are usually more fit than hunters, jumpers or dressage horses; therefore, they can seem thinner compared to these other horses. Event horses have the challenge of settling and concentrating on dressage while they are so fit that they feel like being much more active! I like to see event horses with an oval barrel in the summer and a circular barrel in the winter. Most show horses have a circular barrel year round because they are kept heavier than event horses.

# SUPPLEMENTS

**FAT SUPPLEMENT:** There are many good fat supplements on the market. Make sure you are using one that is nutritionally balanced and bio-available. All horses can benefit from a fat supplement and especially athletes! A great one on the market is Ultimate Finish, made by Buckeye Feeds.

**FREE CHOICE**: *trace mineral salt

*Fresh water, or with 1/4 cup of Apple Cider Vinegar per 5 gallons of water.

## POSSIBLE ADDITIONAL SUPPLEMENTS:

MULTVITAMIN-MINERAL SUPPLEMENT
JOINT SUPPORT SUPPLEMENT
VITAMIN E & SELENIUM
ELECTROLYTES
HOOF SUPPLEMENT

Since supplements are specific to each horse they need to be considered carefully. Some horses have excellent feet and may not need biotin. Instead they may need a probiotic (enzymes) such as Fastrack to help them digest feeds, or other supplements for differing reasons. It is important to individualize each horse's diet to meet his specific needs. I do not advocate the use of a lot of supplements. I am pointing out that some horses don't need supplements, while others need certain ones for certain reasons. All horses should have free access to a trace mineral salt block and fresh water.

You will also find it necessary to use different supplements at different times in the horse's schedule. For example, you could use a vitamin E and selenium supplement to strengthen his immune system a week prior to and following administration of vaccinations. Some horses need extra care to stave off the onset of ulcers as well. All these issues are different reasons for choosing to use supplements.

A fat supplement is important for fat-soluble vitamins to be absorbed, hormone production, and proper nerve function. Fat supplementation can also be helpful in trying to put weight on a horse without adding excess energy. A fat supplement should provide an excellent balance of omega-3, 6, and 9 fatty acids, important in production of hormones, hair and hoof growth. Vitamin E is expensive to add to feeds, so most commercial feeds don't add enough or any at all. The best fat supplement to consider is a commercial grain supplement, which is high in fat but also contains added minerals and vitamins. The Omega-3 fats have shown to act as a natural anti-inflammatory in the body, benefiting any horse in work! Beet pulp mash is also a valued addition to the horse's diet. It is a wonderful fiber for the hind gut, promoting beneficial bacteria and intestinal health.

There are several reasons for adding vinegar to your horse's water. Apple cider vinegar is high in potassium, and it adds flavor to the water, which comes in handy when you want the water away from home to taste like the water at home. You can add the vinegar to the horse's water in his stall and leave him with fresh water out in his paddock. Most horses will like the taste of the apple cider vinegar, and you are only adding a very small amount, mostly for flavor.

Brick size trace mineral blocks can be placed in the feed tubs to discourage bolting of feed. The horse will have to eat grain around the salt block, slowing down the speed at which he eats. This also encourages him to lick the salt block.

A hoof supplement can be used to ensure good hoof growth. Faster hoof growth usually equals healthier hooves.

Only use an iron supplement when a horse is in heavy work. Iron is not commonly deficient in the horse's diet unless he is in heavy work.

A joint supplement can be used to support joints and surrounding tissues. These are important to protect due to the stresses presented during cross-country jumping and dressage. IV and IM joint therapies are also options that have proved themselves in studies.

Selenium is deficient in some soils across the nation, but is excess in others, so test your soil first to know where you stand. Either an excess of selenium in the diet, or a deficiency can cause sore feet and even death in horses; it is very important to know how much selenium your horse is ingesting! The vitamin E and selenium supplement is a preventative for tying-up as well as muscle soreness.

Equine nutrition is a very complex science and becomes extremely important when you start working with horses as athletes rather than pleasure animals. Inform yourself and keep up-to-date on the latest nutrition research.

Electrolytes can be given with each workout feed or added to the horse's water, and are vital in the warmer months. Electrolytes fed daily year round can be beneficial in making your horse drink plenty of water and keeping their gut healthier.

## ELECTROLYTE RECIPE

FOUR PARTS LITE SALT
THREE PARTS TRACE MINERAL SALT
TWO PARTS POWDERED DOLOMITE
ONE PART EPSOM SALTS

Electrolytes are very important for normal metabolic functioning of the horse. The above recipe is a very effective mixture that top endurance riders use. The trace mineral salt provides sodium and other minerals. The Lite Salt provides needed potassium, and the dolomite provides calcium. The Epsom salts provide magnesium. This mix should be given at the rate of one ounce per day and two ounces on the days the horse is worked. Adding an extra ounce in the horse's workout feed is an easy way to manage his electrolyte requirements. The horse's sweat is ten times more concentrated than a human's sweat.

# <u>HOOF CARE</u>

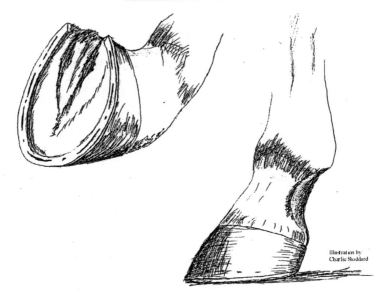

Illustration by
Charlie Stoddard

1) HOOF OIL APPLIED TO THE WHOLE HOOF

2) HOOF SEALER APPLIED TO OUTER WALL

3) SHOD AT LEAST EVERY 6 WEEKS

4) IODINE DROPS APPLIED TO FROGS

5) USE MEDICATED HOOF PACKING FOR:

    A.)FOLLOWING COMPETITION

    B.)EXCESSIVE HAULING TIME

    C.) SORENESS OR HEAT IN FOOT

A good farrier is a must for any horse in competition. Keep your horse on a regular shoeing schedule (some horses need to be shod every 4-5 weeks). You will at some point find the need for using studs, in many cases as early as training level. The use of studs will depend on your horse. You will need to do some research about what types to use and for what conditions. Placement of the studs is very important. Never use different height studs on the same foot or same end of the horse. Be conservative with your studs to prevent injury and always use leg protection if you have studs in place. Using larger studs than necessary will cause the horse's leg to twist as he moves and his foot is held in place with a large stud. This torsion can tear tendons or ligaments.

If the pastures are muddy, and your horse's feet are too soft, consider using a foot rot spray consisting of iodine and alcohol. Iodine drops applied to the frogs after rain can also help keep the frogs healthy and free of thrush. Take into consideration that iodine is very drying; it may be a hindrance if the hoof is too dry already. This is one example of using common sense; if a hoof is so dry that the frog has already cracked, iodine can help kill bacteria introduced into the crack and Ichthammol could be applied on top of it to soothe and protect the tissue.

Use medicated hoof packing for any soreness, during long trailer rides, and following the stadium or cross-country phases of an event. In the stadium and cross-country phases you can pack your horse's hooves with a small amount of packing to cushion the frog and sole. Some examples are: Forshner's Medicated Packing and Hawthorne's Sole Pack. Tender soles may be toughened by using venice turpentine on a regular basis. There are many commercial products available. Talk to your farrier, vet and trainer for other recommendations.

Hoof sealer is an excellent product for the outer hoof wall, as it controls the moisture content of the hoof; helping with cracks, white line disease, and sealing old nail holes. It is important to do everything you can to ensure a strong, healthy hoof. This product also neutralizes the acid in the bedding due to urine, which degrades a horse's hooves. There are several products on the market. Some are sprayed on and some are painted on. Two examples are The Right Step and Tough Stuff. You will have to decide if it is something your horse needs as part of his regular care, or only after he has been shod to seal old nail holes.

Some horses may also benefit once a week from the use of Reducine, a formula that can be applied to the coronary band to increase blood circulation to the hoof, resulting in a healthier hoof.

The hoof oil recipe contains pine tar and neatsfoot oil to protect the hoof from dry and wet conditions. Venice turpentine will toughen the soles of the hoof. Eucalyptis oil has antiseptic properties. This hoof oil mixture is to be applied to the bottom (sole) of the hoof and also the outer hoof wall itself. Many hoof oils could be used, but it is cheaper to make your own mixture, which is more effective.

## BETH'S HOOF OIL:

1qt. VENICE TURPENTINE

1qt. NEATSFOOT OIL

1qt. PINE TAR

2 oz. EUCALYPTIS OIL

# WINTER BLANKETING

**< 50 F** = LIGHT WEIGHT BLANKET

**< 40 F** = MEDIUM WEIGHT BLANKET

**< 30 F** = HEAVY WEIGHT BLANKET

**< 20 F** = HEAVY WEIGHT BLANKET w/ HOOD

**< 10 F** = ADD STRAW TO STALL

**< 0 F** = ADD 24 HOUR HAY AVAILABILITY

* USE A QUARTER-SHEET WHEN WORKING HORSES IN FREEZING TEMPURATURES (less than 32F/ 0C, considering wind chill factors).

Horses need a wardrobe all their own! Fly sheets, anti-sweat sheets, coolers, rain sheets, and winter blankets! I do not blanket in the summer, but winter work for horses can be tricky due to the condition of their coats. If a horse stays blanketed during winter it can be beneficial in retarding their winter coat. A heavy winter coat will cause much extra work for the rider. The horse sweats more during a workout and can take hours of toweling to become dry. And you must always cool the horse out properly!

You could body clip the under-side of the neck, chest, shoulders (as well as a thin path around the hind legs). It is important to leave hair where the tack will be and across the horse's loins and croup for protection and warmth. You may need to body clip twice in the winter, depending upon where you live. Be careful not to allow the horse to become sunburned for at least a couple of weeks following the body clipping (this can happen in winter).

Use a quarter sheet when working horses below 32F, and take extra time warming up their muscles. Tests have shown that working horses in freezing conditions can damage the sensitive tissues in their lungs. You should avoid working your horse when it is below freezing out, or work him in the warmest part of the day and don't work him hard enough to get his respiration rate elevated. Use coolers to keep the horse warm while he is drying following a workout. And rain sheets are needed in the summer as well as winter.

Blanketing requires much extra effort; if you are not willing to put in the time - **<u>do not blanket!</u>** Horses which are not in heavy work in the winter do not need blankets and are better off without them. However, if it is merely the horse's month off between seasons, continue to blanket the horse, because he is going back into conditioning and will have been blanketed for the winter already. It is very important that the blankets are changed twice daily (go by the highs and lows for the day) and the horse must be groomed daily to avoid blanket sores. Blankets must be kept clean. **These points are very important!**

Layering blankets is best for warmth, but never use more than two blankets at a time. The weight of the blankets can be constricting, rubbing off hair or even causing sores. Once the temperature drops below 10F, add a bale of straw to the stall (on top of the usual thick shavings) and offer the horse more hay. If you are unfortunate enough to live where the temperature may drop below zero, you will need to add warmth from within by keeping hay in front of the horse at all times, allowing him to eat as much as he pleases (this is not the time for a diet). You may already offer your horse hay all the time, which is needed for some horses, but not for others. Grass hay has been proven to keep horses warmer than alfalfa; you can still use both in the winter. This program is progressive in nature. As the temperature drops keep adding precautions.

**Never shut the horse up in a barn to keep him warm!!** It is extremely important for horses to always have fresh, outdoor air to breathe, no matter how cold it is! The ammonia in urine is very damaging to a horse's lungs and can cause them to bleed during heavy workouts. This damage is virtually undetectable until the condition is so extreme that blood trickles from the nostrils. Urine fumes (ammonia) can also cause heaves, an incurable lung disease. Never shut all the doors and windows in your barn. Horses are large animals producing large amounts of heat, they will stay warm enough just being in the shelter of the barn and eating hay. Always leave a door or window open for fresh air. Even if you cannot smell the ammonia, your horse can be affected by it. A clean stall is not enough. Hopefully he is in a clean stall to start out the night, but before morning he will need to urinate! This cannot be stressed enough. Horses lungs are far more sensitive than ours and much larger. The best situation is an open door off the back of the stall, allowing the horse to walk outside for fresh air. Think about how much warmer you are when you are moving around in the cold rather than being forced to stand in one spot. Horses are the same, they are big animals that produce large amounts of heat, and keep themselves warm by walking around!

# VET AND WORMING
# SCHEDULE

JANUARY 15: PASTEWORM COMBOCARE

MARCH 26: PASTEWORM IVERMECTIN

JUNE 5: PASTEWORM STRONGID

JULY 5: PASTEWORM COMBOCARE

SEPTEMBER 25: PASTEWORM IVERMECTIN

DECEMBER 15: PASTEWORM STRONGID

- COGGINS ANNUALLY & HEALTH CERTIFICATE AS NEEDED

- TEETH CHECKED TWICE A YEAR

- VACCINES GIVEN PER VET'S RECOMMENDATIONS FOR YOUR SHOW SCHEDULE & AREA

The worming schedule I have chosen rotates some of the different chemical classes of wormers that are currently on the market. I am a firm believer in worming throughout the winter months, no matter how cold it is where you live. Worming programs differ all over the country; use a vet recommended program for your area if you have any questions.

The ComboCare Gel is effective for 84 days because it kills encysted eggs in the intestinal lining. It contains 2% Moxidectin and 12.5% Praziquantel and is effective against large strongyles, small strongyles, pinworms, hairworms, stomach worms, ascarids, bots, encysted small strongles, and tapeworms.

Ivermectin Paste contains 1.87% Ivermectin and is effective against large strongyles, small strongyles, pinworms, hairworms, threadworms, stomachworms, lungworms, ascarids, and bots.

Strongid Paste contains Pyrantel Pamoate and is effective against large strongyles, small strongyles, pinworms, and hairworms.

These three paste wormers cover all the worms that threaten your horse's health. If your horse lives in an over crowded pasture with other horses you may want to use a more aggressive worming program. This schedule should keep a horse worm free if he is grazing individually in his own two-acre pasture. When in doubt, get a fecal test done to check for worms or worm eggs in your horse's manure. It is advisable to use a probiotic supplement for a week following each paste worming. This will help to re-establish the beneficial bacteria in your horse's gut! Each horse will choose an area where he will go to defecate most of the time, allowing the rest of his pasture to be used for fresh grazing. This makes it very easy to pick their lots out at least weekly, helping to control flies and worms.

# VACCINATIONS FOR HIGH RISK HORSES

| VACCINATION | | SHOW HORSES |
|---|---|---|
| Influenza | Intranasal | 3 per year |
| Rhinopneumonitis | | 3 per year |
| Encephalomyelitis | | 2 per year |
| Tetanus | | 2 per year |
| Potomac Horse Fever | | 2 per year |
| Streptococcus equii | Intranasal | 1 per year |
| Rabies | | 1 per year |
| Botulism | | 1 per year |
| EPM | | 1per year |

A good equine vet will play a large role in your conditioning program. You need to follow an entire program that will reduce the chance of re-infestation of worms by preventing pastures from becoming horse-poor. There are many management techniques for worm control: keeping stalls and dry lots picked out daily; spreading manure rather than piling it; never spreading the manure in an area where horses will be grazing; using harrows to scatter piles in pastures on a regular basis; using an effective fly control system; proper pasture size; rotating pastures and so on.

You may choose to have an equine dentist take care of your horse's teeth. Some horses need to have their teeth checked more often than once per year and you need to look out for those tell tale signs of chewing or bit acceptance problems.

The annual exam should also include necessary vaccines (and boosters) along with a thorough sheath cleaning (if needed). It is important to let your vet know your horse's travel plans when considering vaccines. The schedule above is for high-risk horses, which includes horses in competition (show horses). Advice for vaccine schedules change as new knowledge becomes available, so use the table I have provided as a guideline and check with your vet for any recommended changes. A horse traveling to different areas to compete should to be current on all his vaccinations to avoid illness. I prefer to spread out the administration of vaccines and give them individually.

The vet will need to prepare a Coggins test at least once per year. Some events require the Coggins to be done within six months. Your travel plans will play a part in your need for a health certificate as well. You are required to have a health certificate if you travel across state lines for any reason. The certificate is only valid for one month, so you may need one filled out every month by a vet, if you are crossing state lines that often. Programs are being developed for show horses to have passports between states in order to avoid a monthly health certificate. Check with your vet to find out what options are in your area!

# Complete Blood Panel

An annual blood panel test and fecal test should be done by your vet to check for levels in the blood and worm larvae in the horse's feces. These tests could be done prior to the new competition season and should be repeated if any problems are found, after a course of action was carried out to solve the problem. The fecal tests will tell you if your worming schedule is sufficient. The CBP (complete blood panel) is a test measuring the horse's blood chemistry. This test can indicate a malfunctioning liver, kidney, heart, hydration levels, or inflammation in the body earlier than signs of these problems are detectable in the horse. There are approximately twenty-four parameters measured. Selenium isn't included, though it is important for it to be measured annually. Many questions can be answered with a CBP as well. Is the horse ingesting the proper amount of electrolytes, selenium, or protein? Are the horse's body systems keeping up with his workload? A CBP could be beneficial in telling you why the horse's heart rate has been abnormally high after the last few workouts, when you observed no other indicators.

# __BATHING CARE__

__SHAMPOO__ : QUALITY SHAMPOO, ¼ CUP

OF PROVIDONE/IODINE SCRUB and ½ CUP

OF EPSOM SALTS MIXED INTO FIVE

GALLONS OF WARM WATER

__*LEAVE ON RINSE__ :

16 oz WITCH HAZEL

16 oz APPLE CIDER VINEGAR

8 oz CONDITIONER

 * MIX INGREDIENTS and USE 1/2 CUP PER

TWO GALLONS OF WARM RINSE WATER.

* ADD THREE TABLESPOONS OF IODINE

TINCTURE PER TWO GALLONS OF RINSE

WATER IF NEEDED (to control fungus growth)


+ BATHE WEEKLY and RINSE DAILY

DURING WARM WEATHER (> 70F)


+ CLEAN SHEATH OR NIPPLES DURING

WEEKLY BATH

Regular bathing is important to clean the sweat and dirt from the horse's skin; a daily rinse off cannot replace this critical bath. A bath can be given weekly if the weather permits, but should not be done more often. The bath is also worthless if it is not done thoroughly, using a rubber curry and mitt to get the horse scrubbed clean all over. Built up dirt can cause girth galls, saddles sores, scratches, scabs, rain rot, etc., all of which will cause a disruption in your training schedule. Daily use of curries, mitts, hard and soft brushes, are also very important in achieving that healthy, glowing coat we all admire.

Use warm water in bathing to help loosen oil and dirt. Adding Epsom salts to the bath water can help soften the water, which will help get the horse cleaner. You can also add Betadine Scrub for it's antiseptic properties. You may choose any quality shampoo, as long as it has easy rinsing properties. One cannot stress enough the importance of getting all the soap out of the horse's coat and tail. Distilled vinegar is very helpful for rinsing out soap from the horse's skin. In a five-gallon bucket of warm rinse water, you could add a ½ cup of vinegar. After rinsing well with plain water, put a bucket of warm water with the "leave on conditioner" all over the horse. This helps to replace oils in the coat, keeping a soft, shiny coat. You could use a homemade mixture that is listed above, which needs a lot of shaking before adding to your rinse water. If you are encountering any skin problems at all, it is a good idea to add iodine to the rinse water. Do not wash off the rinse mixture, simply scrape off horse and towel down. Most barns have water heaters in the wash stall, supplying them with warm water. If you do not have access to warm water in your barn, a portable heater that simply plugs into an outlet and is dropped into a five gallon bucket of water is available. I use one of these to travel with, and they are very nice for shows.

Clean geldings, stallions and mares with sheath cleanser. It is excellent for cleaning between mares' nipples as well as the sheaths on the males. Be sure to rinse well. Warm water will be much appreciated by your fine friend!

Daily spraying with tepid water to remove sweat out of a horse's coat is important in warm weather. Follow this with a sponging of warm water, which may contain recommended amounts of liniment and a cup of witch hazel per five gallons. The winter months do not allow for rinsing, so a fair amount of grooming needs to be done following the workout. If it is at least sixty degrees out, you may want to bathe their legs and tail. A heated wash area is invaluable during the winter, allowing you to bathe your horse more often and him to dry more quickly. Cold hydrotherapy following a jumping or galloping workout is more difficult in the winter. Ice boots could still be used as well as a rub down with liniment.

# What if I board my horse?

Even if you board your horse you can still have control of his management situation. Inquire about keeping your horse in an individual lot, or with only one other horse, that is at least a few acres. You can graze your horse for long periods of time before and after riding him. You can offer to do the soil samples yourself from your horse's pasture. Maybe other boarders would be willing to split the cost of applying lime to the pasture. A clean up day could be organized once a week to clean up manure out of the pasture. Offer to mow the pasture if weeds are out of control or the grass is over eight inches.

Smart Pak is a wonderful option for boarders. They package supplements in daily dosages with your horse's name on it, making it very easy to add to your horse's feed. If the barn you board with doesn't add supplements at all, you can give your horse a workout feed and add all his supplements to it everyday you work him. You can send grass, hay and grain samples to be tested to help determine what supplements your horse may need. Your Complete Blood Panel will also be of great benefit.

If the barn you board with only feeds one type of hay, several supplements are on the market to use in cases where only alfalfa is fed or only grass hay is fed. If you want to supplement with alfalfa, because your horse is only getting grass hay and grass in his pasture, there are many choices. Alfalfa is sold in bales, cubes and pellets. You could offer your horse alfalfa as a workout feed for the extra protein and minerals it contains. This can help keep your horse from tying up because he is receiving extra protein after you have worked him and he would not get it on his day off.

Some boarding barns change out horses' blankets and some don't. You are better off not to blanket your horse if you can't change it twice a day with the lows and highs for the day. If your barn doesn't change out blankets, and you still want to blanket you horse, maybe a trade could be worked out. Another option would be to have a light blanket on the horse during the day, and you could add a blanket on top in the evenings. Then someone at the barn could pull off the top blanket in the mornings. This all depends on the climate and your situation. Work with the other boarders as well. Maybe some are available in the mornings and others available in the evenings;

all of you could work together to make a blanketing schedule.

A few options are also available if your barn doesn't have a hot water heater. Would all the boarders be willing to get one installed? Individual bucket heaters are also available that drop down into a bucket of water and plug into an outlet. They typically take 15 to 20 minutes to make five gallons of water fairly warm. These can make the water hot, so be mindful of the time they are left in the bucket. Portable water heaters are also available, though they are more expensive. Maybe a few boarders would want to share one!

Boarding your horse doesn't lock you into certain plans. Work with your barn manager and the other boarders. Offer to build jumps and cavalletti for the ring or field. Take an interest in the farm your horse lives on; it will benefit you in the long run. If all else fails, living in the country with your horse is the most rewarding experience I can imagine!!

# <u>EVENT CONDITIONING</u>

# <u>TECHNIQUES</u>

The first four levels are preparatory levels for the actual conditioning for the Novice level of Eventing. They are meant to be executed for one month each. After spending the proper time on the first four levels you are ready to compete in the beginner novice level. The last four levels coincide with the actual competition levels of Eventing and are meant to be executed for a year each.

These conditioning levels are designed to be a guide – a sort of outline for conditioning. You must use an experienced eye to know if you need to spend more time in certain areas. You may need a trainer to help you determine if your horse is fit enough for your level of competition. If a horse has had a few weeks off (for his winter month off or a soreness), resume his conditioning program with one week through each lower level, then settle into the schedule for his current level of competition. **These are only guidelines.** Try to be conservative and generous in allowing conditioning and healing time. These schedules are in preparation for horse trials. Preparation for a Three-day event would take more conditioning for the endurance (roads and tracks) phases.

A horse's muscular system will show the effects of conditioning in a matter of weeks. The respiratory system takes a few months to become conditioned. The horse's tendons, ligaments and joints require several months to become conditioned. Finally, the hooves and bones take up to a year. This means the horse will feel like he is more fit than he really is – which is very important to keep in mind to avoid injuries! He will want to be more active in his training than he should be. Because the muscular and respiratory systems will be conditioned before the tendons, ligaments and bones the horse will feel very fit. It is at this point people may be tempted to move ahead in the horse's conditioning schedule too soon, causing an injury. He may be feeling fresh before each workout, but do not let that fool you into moving ahead too soon. Check the horse's pulse before, during and after each workout, as well as after recovery every day.

Check his legs and feet for heat or swelling daily.
These facts are the main reason I feel it is important to
spend a year competing in each level of eventing
before moving on to the next level. Within a year at a
given level a horse should be going clean (without time
or jumping faults in both jumping phases) at their
competitions. If you are having trouble going clean, in
either the cross-country or the stadium phase by the
middle of your competition season, you need to
evaluate your horse's abilities. Are you interfering
with your horse's performance? Is your horse not
athletic enough to perform what is being asked of him?
These are important questions to ask yourself and your
trainer. If you find that you are not confident and
competent at a certain level, you must stop competing
and go back to training or competing at a lower level.
Even if you qualify to compete at the level you are
having trouble with. Go back to the basics and work
on strengthening your flat work, balancing you and
your horse through all the phases, and improving your
seat. If you find you have trouble in an area, take the
time to find the problem, learn from it, and fix it. If
you fail to take this time, pressing ahead anyway could
cost you your life or your horse's life in a bad accident

on course. **Eventing can be a dangerous sport, but it doesn't have to be!**

If you are breaking a horse to take all the way through the levels of eventing, you should follow these guidelines:

**Age 2** - break the horse with minimal amount of riding, many days off, use long walks and much ground driving. Refrain from working the horse two days in a row. The horse is still growing so do not stress his joints. Do not work him in a circle less than twenty meters.

**Age 3** - spend time on dressage basics, long walks, never working more than 15 minutes a day in the dressage ring. Again, refrain from working the horse two days in a row. The horse is not done growing, do not work him in a smaller circle than twenty meters.

**Age 4** - spend one month with each of the first four levels, then work on them for the rest of the year. Gymnastic jumping must be progressive in nature, very minimal in height, this is a confidence building time. The horse could be introduced to competing in the beginner novice level later in this year.

**Age 5** - spend this year introducing the horse to small shows while working on the novice level of eventing.

The horse could be competed about one novice trial per month with a small dressage show, hunter show, or clinic in between.

**Age 6** - advance to the training level in eventing, competing ten months of the season, using clinics, dressage shows and schooling jumper divisions to further the education and experience of the horse. I like to schedule an outing every other weekend.

**Age 7** – move on to the preliminary level. Follow the same competition schedule as the previous year.

**Age 8** – the intermediate level in eventing.

**Age 9** - advanced level of eventing.

This schedule is conservative in that it gives the horse one year at each level of eventing. This is important in order to give the horse a chance to solve many different problems on the cross-country courses at the lower fence heights. By the time the horse is faced with complex problems at the upper levels he has the experience and confidence to take the jumps safely. It takes years of continual conditioning to create a top athlete for this sport. Every year you spend conditioning the horse properly allows him to build stronger bones and supporting tissues. This outline is left open for much customizing, certain horses may need to repeat certain levels of competition if they are finding the current level of too difficult or strenuous. Riders may need to repeat a year at a level if they lack the confidence to move on as well.

Warmbloods or heavier breeds (other than pure thoroughbreds) may want to start the whole schedule a year later due to their slower growth rates. Many breeds other than pure thoroughbreds will have a harder time getting in shape than the thoroughbred. These horses may need more strong trotting, added gallops (not adding speed, just time) or they may need a few more minutes added to each gymnastic jumping day. The warmblood with his heavy bones can break down easily with the extra weight pounding on his joints, so be careful not to pound his legs while you are giving him extra work. Extra hill work is wonderful for added conditioning with any horse, though some riders do not have hills available to them. If you have hills available to you, use them and spend less time with the gallops. The hills should be trotted or cantered up and walked down. Spend some time at the top of the hill allowing the horse to walk out a bit before heading back down. Learn how to use your hills and incorporate them into your conditioning schedule.

Give one month off at the end of the season. Then spend a week working the horse at each level to attain condition for the next level of the following season. When the schedule says go back to spend a week training at each level, it means all the way back to the very first level of lunging to practice stretching techniques. For example, if you spent the previous year competing in Novice, you will need to spend a week at each level (five weeks) before starting the conditioning program for the Training level. The month off is usually December, since that is the first month of the competition year. But that is determined by the horse's situation and his competition schedule. The month off should be spent with the horse turned out and allowed to be a horse. This month off is for his mind as well as his body. This schedule will allow the horse to begin conditioning work at his new level approximately two months before the first event of that season. If you feel the need for it, I encourage you to compete at your previous level for the first event of the season (in the open division, of course). If you feel confident and competent, go ahead and compete at the next level, assuming you meet the requirements. I encourage you to have schooled a few different cross-country courses at the level you intend to compete, before actual competition. This will allow both you and the horse to experience the challenges of the fences at the next level, before you are trying to avoid time penalties.

This brings up a good point. Be sure you place safety and security before your time requirements, no matter what the competition! If the conditions are bad, whether it be footing or weather, throw the time requirements out the window and always consider the horse's safety first. It is one thing to go out there and try to kill yourself; it is completely up to you. But you are responsible for your horse's well-being, and he trusts you to do the right thing for him. He will go too fast in bad footing just because you ask him; it is what you have trained him to do. If he falls because you ask him to do something he should not be asked to do, it will shake his confidence and he may never trust you again. The whole sport of eventing is based on trust between you and your mount; don't let him down. No ribbon is worth it!

The equine athlete must have special considerations concerning care of their legs also. They must be set up (wrapped) under certain conditions and looked after daily. Cold leg therapy accompanied by a rub down with linament following each workout is one of my preventative therapies. You can mix the strong linaments with rubbing alcohol to reduce the chance of blistering the horse. It also reduces the cost if you are using it everyday. Each workout should include splint and ankle boots with bell boots on the horse's front feet. Bell boots could be taken off in the stadium ring to allow a sloppy horse to feel the sting of a hit, but never school cross-country without them. Be careful to protect the horse's feet and legs at all times. Wrap the legs with poultices on the evenings following gallops or hard jumping work. These are preventative measures and you will have to decide for yourself how to best approach them.

# LEVEL ONE

**WEEK ONE**: LUNGE 15 MIN. W/ SIDE
REINS @ TROT
TROT CAVALLETI 15 MIN.

**WEEK TWO**: LUNGE W/ SR 15 MIN. @
TROT & 8 MIN. @ CANTER
 15 MIN. TROT & CANTER CIRCLES W/ 2
 CAV. AT ENDS

**WEEK THREE**: LUNGE W/SR 15 MIN. @
TROT & 10 MIN. @ CANTER
15 MIN. TROT & CAN. CIRCLES W/ 2 CAV.
AT ENDS

**WEEK FOUR**: LUNGE W/ SR 15 MIN. @
TROT & 15 MIN. @ CANTER
 15 MIN. CANTER CAV. (3 POLES, 9 FEET
APART)

DAY 1: OUT ON TRAILS (30 minutes)

DAY 2: DAY OFF

DAY 3: WORK OUT

DAY 4: OUT ON TRAILS (30 minutes)

DAY 5: WORKOUT

DAY 6: DAY OFF

DAY 7: WORKOUT

The minutes in each of the levels in this book are not intended for the rider to work on the proposed exercise for the entire time given. The time expressed is meant to include other work with the horse while working on these exercises. Level one is meant to teach the horse to stretch down towards the bit and stretch the muscles in his back and neck. As you are lunging the horse, keep him stretching down in front and moving from behind so he is stepping into the bit. Do not allow him too much playfulness during lunging, injury can result. Side reins will discourage horseplay during lunging. **During lunging, interject one minute of walking per five minutes of trotting; and one minute of walking per four minutes of cantering. This is to be carried out any time the horse is on the lunge line or round pen.** These small breaks will help prevent injuries and build up the horse's hind end with the transitions. Include the time spent walking in the total time of the trot or canter exercise.

I do not agree with excess lunging of the horse, but this is the only level which requires it and never for more than 30 minutes at a time, including breaks. **The best way to lunge is free-lunge in a large round pen**

**so you are never pulling on the horse. This can help prevent injuries associated with lunging. It is wise to take frequent walk breaks and change directions often when lunging.** The lunging in this level offers the young or fresh horse a chance to expend some energy before being mounted, which can be beneficial in avoiding the formation of bad habits. Always remove the side reins before mounting and use a steady, quiet, soft hand to replace them!

The cavalleti work can vary a bit more. It is meant to be carried out with the horse mounted. The height of the cavalletti should be about 15-20 cm. A proper cavalletti can be built and then be used for gymnastic jumping. Another option is to use large poles, such as telephone poles, which would be 15 cm in height. The cavalletti need to be 2 ft 8 in to 3 ft 4 in apart for the walk, depending on the size of the horse's stride. For the trot, the cavalletti need to be at a distance of 4 ft to 4 ft 6 in. At a canter the cavalletti should be 9 ft apart. Not more than four, and not less than three cavalletti in a row should be used, it is important not to drill the horse over them more than 15 minutes. You don't want to make the horse sour, sore or bored. **I suggest you be mounted for the cavalleti**

**work, and remain in a two-point position going through the cavalletti.**

Be sure to give the horse his days off each week. Never skimp on his trail ride. This is a time for the two of you to bond and have some fun. Just don't mention to the horse that the trail ride is supposed to introduce new environments in a relaxed atmosphere. Keep the horse on the bit, moving forward at a walk throughout the trail ride. We are still trying to build muscles through his neck and back. Always use the trail ride to your advantage. If the horse spooks at something use your voice to calm him and your leg pressure to make him keep moving in the desired direction. This reinforces teaching him to move away from your leg, while also teaching him to trust your voice. This early reinforcement of the aids can be very useful when you are on the cross-country course and he starts to shy from the next fence, or anything else for that matter.

Going to the next level – is the horse walking, trotting and cantering rhythmically through the cavalletti? If not, work at this level until he is.

# LEVEL ONE GYMNASTICS

Set up some permanent cavalletti that you can use everyday in warm-up and cool-down sessions. I use telephone poles as my permanent cavalletti. The distance between the cavalletti will vary depending on the length of your horse's stride. Start with an approximate distance and then set the distance to the comfort level of the horse.

I I I I

Walk through cavalletti ~ 3 feet apart.

I I I I

Trot through cavalletti ~ 4 feet apart.

I   I   I

Canter through cavalletti ~ 9 feet apart.

**LEGEND:**

I = Cavalletti

X = Cross Rail Jump

1 = Vertical Jump

H = Oxer Jump

# LEVEL TWO

**WEEK ONE**: 20 MIN.  CIRCLES &
DIAGONALS

**WEEK TWO**: 20 MIN.  TROT & CANTER
TRANSITIONS

**WEEK THREE**: 20 MIN.  TROT & CANTER
SPIRALS

**WEEK FOUR**: 20 MIN.  TROT & CANTER, 5
MIN.  SIT-TROT TRAN.

DAY 1: OUT ON TRAILS (45 minutes)
DAY 2: DAY OFF
DAY 3: 1/2 WORKOUT W/ GYMNASTIC
JUMPING
DAY 4: OUT ON TRAILS (45 minutes)
DAY 5: WORKOUT
DAY 6: DAY OFF
DAY 7: WORKOUT

The work time in this level is not asking you to circle the horse for 20 min. at the trot. The guideline is to include circles at the trot and canter with an approximate total of 20 min. of trot and canter by the end of your workout. Level two is designed to teach the horse to bend properly. It is important to do the proper warm-up exercises prior to your beginning the workout. A few minutes of walking and trotting in a long and low frame in 20 meter circles while changing directions should be used to warm up and cool down the horse. The circles and diagonals should be broken up into differing directions with many breaks (walking on a long rein). The total length of this workout, including warm-up, breaks and warm-down, should not be longer than thirty minutes. When the horse bends well, doing what you ask, give him a small walk break, rewarding him with your voice and dropping your reins. Keep in mind you are asking the horse to use muscles he has not built up, you can make him sore by drilling him over and over. **A sore horse will soon become a sour horse!**

The trot and canter transitions are meant to build up the horse's back and hind end muscles. It is important to take this time to stay soft with your hands and teach the horse to make his transitions according to the position of your seat. If you are very consistent in deepening your seat as you ask for a downward transition, he will quickly learn to make a downward transition as you deepen your seat. This is very important in keeping his mouth soft and his mind open. Change directions and transitions often, staying as quite and balanced as possible. Again it is important to reward him with your voice, taking small breaks where he is encouraged to stretch his neck down and out.

At this level you want to introduce spirals as a bending/ balancing exercise. Only spiral in and out at even intervals, with the horse properly bent. If the horse is unable to stay balanced throughout the exercise, you are asking too much of him, or you are doing it improperly. Don't practice it wrong - horses learn from repetition! Get a good dressage instructor and learn how to do it correctly. Start with a 20m circle, get the horse balanced, use your legs to guide and support him into a 15m circle. This is a small enough spiral for now. Keep the horse bent properly as you spiral out to your 20m circle. This is accomplished at the trot first, then the canter. Give the horse a break between each completed spiral exercise. Proper balance, rhythm, and bend should be maintained throughout the exercise, although at this level you can not expect it.

If you are not able to sit a horse's trot properly you need to learn, to avoid being hard on your horse's back. This exercise is meant to incorporate the sit trot into your work by transitioning it in and out of your trot, canter and walk. Only sit the trot for a minute, then transition to something else. The horse needs to build back muscles to carry you in a sitting trot, so be patient.

You will be introducing **gymnastic jumping (18" high)** at this level, you will also need to vary the exercises. The goal is to teach the horse how to balance and handle himself over fences. Start out with simple gymnastics, trotting the horse through the cavalletti to a small cross pole fence at the end. The distance will be determined by your mount's stride. Then graduate to trotting the cavalletti, cantering a cross pole and then cantering over one cavalletti placed after the jump. Placing the cavalletti before the jumps will help the horse learn to balance himself before the fence, it can be very beneficial to horses that rush their fences. Placing the cavalletti after the jump can teach a horse to balance himself after the jump and can help with horses that tend to rush after the jump. I graduate the horse slowly, adding differing combinations. Use a single cavalletti before a combination and after a combination. Graduate the horse to a point of setting up a line of five strides, then asking them to do it in five or six strides, depending on how much you shorten or lengthen their stride. If the horse rushes through combinations or lines, you will need to place a cavalletti inside the in-and-out or after and before each fine through the combination. A cavalletti can be placed in the middle of the in-and-out, forcing the horse to look where he is landing and take one stride over the cavalletti; then he must place his feet properly before taking off again. Set up jumps to have the horse change leads over the jump with his change of direction. Use jumps set up on circles and cavalletti set up on a circle, then slowly progress to serpentines. It is important to introduce each new exercise slowly until the horse gets the idea. Trot every exercise before cantering it, if possible. Trotting the fences quite a bit in the beginning of the horse's career; there is no need to rush him. Stay in a two-point throughout your gymnastic exercises. Do not get ahead or behind the horse's motion. You are an important aspect of his balance. Keep your body still and let him do the jumping. You will have to go by the size of stride your mount has. The most important thing to remember is the distance between the placing of the jump and the cavalletti. If it is too short or too long you could cause an accident, mistrust, or a strain. Get riding instruction and read books. There are many books on gymnastic jumping. Progress into combinations slowly (take a year if you can) and never drill the horse; allow plenty of walk breaks between lines and fences. **Be careful not to overdo it. There is always another day, but not always another horse!**

At the end of this level your horse should be able to make smooth transitions from canter to trot, not perfect – just smooth is to be expected for now. You have a long time to make it perfect! The spirals are not expected to be tight or balanced yet, but the horse should be able to move away from your leg slightly on a circle. Can you adjust his stride between two cavalletti about 70 feet apart? Can you sit the trot a few minutes at a time? Dressage takes years to perfect and these exercises are just in an infant phase. Do not expect too much at this level.  If the horse has an idea of what you are asking, that is enough for now!

# SAMPLE GYMNASTIC EXERCISES

# FOR LEVEL TWO

I ----------------------- 70 FEET ----------------------- I

Canter over cavalletti approximately 70 feet apart,
counting the strides between them. Practice shortening
and lengthening your horse's stride to alter the number
of strides cantered between the cavaletti.

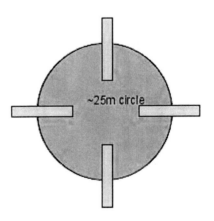

Set up four cavalletti per diagram and practice walking,
trotting, then cantering in a balanced circle over the
cavalletti. Keep your circle at least 25 meters.

# I I I I X

Set four caveletti to your horse's trot distance, then set
up an 18 inch cross rail jump approximately 9 feet after
the last cavalletti (the middle of the cross rail should
be 18 inches). Trot through the exercise and canter
away from the cross rail. Again, make sure your horse
is comfortable with the distance. If he is rushing to
make the jump, you may need to shorten the distance
to the fence. If he is cramped coming to the cross rail,
you will need to lengthen the distance to the jump.
Keep a steady balanced rhythm through the exercise
and stay still on the horse's back with a soft rein. Keep
the horse in the middle of the line the whole way
through the exercise.

# LEVEL THREE

**WEEK ONE**: 30 MIN.  TROT & CANTER W/
FULL & HALF HALTS

**WEEK TWO**: 30 MIN.  TROT & CANT.
LENGTHENING & SHORTENING

**WEEK THREE**: 20 MIN.  TROT W/ LEG
YIELDS, 10 MIN. CANTER

**WEEK FOUR**: 20 MIN. TROT W/ LEG
YIELDS & 10 MIN. CANTER


DAY 1: OUT ON TRAILS (one hour)

DAY 2: DAY OFF

DAY 3: 1/2 WORKOUT W/ GYMNASTIC
JUMPING

DAY 4: OUT ON TRAILS (one hour)

DAY 5: WORKOUT

DAY 6: DAY OFF

DAY 7: WORKOUT

Level three is meant to teach the horse how to compress and collect. The first week is concentrating on the use of full and half halts as an exercise to teach the horse collection. Do not frustrate the horse by too much drilling, but practice your full and half halts at the walk, trot and canter. I once heard Robert Dover at a clinic say, "The half halt is an addition, rather than a subtraction, to your ride." The point is to keep the impulsion through the half halt and into the halt. Remember that a horse at a halt can have impulsion.

After teaching the horse light compression techniques, the next step is to practice lengthening as well. The goal is to lengthen and shorten the stride at all three gaits while keeping the horse on the bit, remaining at the same rhythm and level of impulsion. A good exercise is to lengthen across the diagonal or down the long sides of the dressage ring, then shorten their stride across the short ends of your ring. There are many different exercises and variations; I suggest you practice all of them and learn the proper ways of carrying them out.

Leg yielding may already be part of your warm-up at this point, if not, you need to start teaching it. It is important again not to expect too much. Once a few steps are done correctly, give generous praise and let it be clear to the horse what you are asking of him. Don't move on to shoulder-in until you have mastered leg yielding. It is best to teach the horse lateral movement from the ground by pushing him over with your hand, then once mounted you can replace your hand with your leg. Lateral movement helps strengthen supporting muscles of chest, shoulders, stifles and hindquarters.

The gymnastic jumping at this stage should become a bit more demanding. Include jumps set up in a large circle, always keep the horse straight over the jumps, and in the middle of the jumps. The height of the gymnastic jumps should not exceed **1 ft 9 in** at this level . Your goal is to teach the horse how to jump many different gymnastics, to teach him how to use his body, not how to jump higher. A horse cannot handle a larger fence until he has gained confidence and skill by jumping many gymnastic jumps. Read about different exercises you can use to accomplish this! Use a jump at the end of your cavalletti, in the middle, and before the cavaletti. Give the horse room to return to a trot after a jump if the cavaletti are set up to trot through. Use one stride and two stride in and outs, light in outs, etc., with cavalletti in, before, and after. **Do not scare the horse.** Graduate to more difficult exercises very slowly. It is most important at this stage to encourage the horse, to make jumping fun. The horse's first impression of jumping must be a good one and can make a horse either a willing, bold jumper, or a sour quitter. Never let the horse quit! It is that simple; he should know that it is not ever an option. Give praise after every jump and do not over drill the horse. Jumping is natural for horses and most of them enjoy it, unless the experience has been ruined. Your main goal is to instill confidence in the horse!

Before you move on to the next level be sure you can halt in and out of transitions, carry out a half-halt at the walk, trot and canter. You will also need to leg-yield at the trot. Be sure the horse is comfortable through his gymnastic exercises and course jumping.

# SAMPLE GYMNASTIC EXERCISES FOR

## LEVEL THREE

# I I I I X  X

Set up exercise as previously, adding another cross rail jump 18 feet after the first one.

# I I I I X  1

Set up exercise as previously, changing the last cross rail to a vertical.

# I I I I X  H

Set up exercise as previously, changing the vertical to a small oxer.  Set your oxer up with the back pole 3 inches higher than the front pole and only 18 inches between the poles.

Change the direction you approach and exit the exercises. Alternate stopping on a straight line, turning left, turning right or circling following the exercises. This teaches the horse to listen to you for direction following each jump. Again, keep the horse straight and balanced through the line. Your body should stay as still as possible with a soft, following hand. These are important points throughout the levels for all your gymnastic work.

# LEVEL FOUR TO
# BEGINNER NOVICE

**WEEK ONE**: 1/2 HR TROT/WLK/TROT & 10 MIN. CANTER/WLK/CANTER

**WEEK TWO**: 1/2 HR TROT LEG YIELDS & 10 MIN. CANTER LEG YIELDS

**WEEK THREE**: 1/2 HR TROT EXERCISES & 15 MIN. COUNTER CANTERS

**WEEK FOUR**: 1/2 HR TROT-BACK-TROT & 15 MIN. CANT.-BACK-CANT.

DAY 1: OUT ON TRAILS (one hour thirty minutes)

DAY 2: DAY OFF

DAY 3: 1/2 WORKOUT W/ GYMNASTIC JUMPING

DAY 4: OUT ON TRAILS (one hour thirty minutes)

DAY 5: WORKOUT

DAY 6: DAY OFF

DAY 7: WORKOUT

Level four is the last of the preparatory levels; it is meant to strengthen the horse. Do not drill the horse on any one exercise for a half-hour. That is not how the schedule is to be carried out! Use the schedule to help you know what exercises to introduce into the work, and by the end of the week, be able to carry out. Transitions are used to strengthen the horse's hind end and back muscles. Leg yielding at the canter is introduced to teach the horse balance through lateral movement at the canter. This movement is important because it will be needed later on jump courses to help with speed of turns and placing yourself in the middle of each jump.

The counter canter can be effective in balancing a horse's canter and should be practiced with the horse bent in both directions. It is important to give the horse plenty of room; do not rush him. Never make less than a twenty-meter circle with the counter canter at this early stage. Again, do not drill the horse on counter-canter for 15 minutes. The time frame includes walking breaks, cantering into the change of direction, etc. Use common sense. You should not drill a horse on any one exercise for longer than a few minutes at a time. Sometimes that is too long. **Much**

**encouragement is needed while teaching the horse these new exercises.** Don't worry if he switches his leads or breaks his stride; it is to be expected. Pet the horse for his effort and walk him back to your starting point. Reward him with your voice as you bend him into a circle, opposite of his lead. You will also have to support him with your leg and pet him for his efforts. **Learn how to do counter-canters properly before you try to teach them to a horse!**

Rein-backs can be used to collect the horse and to further the development of his hind end, as well as soften the horse by keeping him supple. This will only work if the rider is very soft, asking the horse with his seat rather than with the reins. This is another one of those exercises that will frustrate the horse very quickly if too many demands are made of him. Be generous with your rewards and never overdo. Incorporate this exercise throughout your ride. Ask for a rein-back when the horse is least expecting it. Just do it gently. Do not back more than a couple of steps.

At this point, the gymnastic jumping should be going smoothly, the horse should have the skills and confidence to be doing many different combinations with the lower fences. Never rush the horse. If there are certain combinations he has trouble with, work it out before raising the jumps. When your horse is going well, increase the **gymnastic jumping to two feet** and keep practicing many different combinations.

If you are breaking a horse or starting a horse over fences, you should spend the rest of the year practicing these levels and not moving on to the novice level until next year. There are many reasons: to give the horse time to develop important system conditioning before going on to track work, to refine the horse's jumping skills, and to spend the important hours in the dressage ring deepening his understanding of dressage basics. This produces a horse who is accepting the bit well and has a bold confidence in jumping. This could also be a good year to finish with a few competitions at the Beginner Novice level. If this is a feasible goal for you, prepare him by going out in the field to hop over a few natural logs or low brush. No need to push him, and keep it fun. The Beginner Novice cross-country course could be trotted the whole way and be encouraging the whole time. This is a great time to get the inexperienced horse out in the late summer and fall for a few horse trials. Don't overdo your schedule or your shows. Let this be a relaxed time for the horse to explore the excitement of the competition world!

# SAMPLE GYMNASTIC EXERCISES

# FOR LEVEL FOUR

## I

Set up a simple cavalletti in the middle of your ring
and practice cantering over it from both directions,
then practice changing directions and changing leads
while cantering figure eights over the cavalletti.

## I I I I X 1 1

Set up as previous exercise with a vertical 18 feet after
the cross rail and another vertical 20 feet after the first.
Your jumps should be 2 feet at this level.

# I I I I X 1 H

Change the last vertical into a small oxer. This oxer
can be up 21 inches wide.

# NOVICE LEVEL

1.) **TRACK WORK** :

1 MILE WALK

1 MILE TROT

1 MILE CANTER

* 1/2 MILE EACH DIRECTION PER

GAIT IN A LONG AND LOW

FRAME

2.) **WARM-UP**: 10 MIN.

GYMNASTIC DRESSAGE

3.) **20 MIN.** JUMPING OR

DRESSAGE WORK (SEE

SCHEDULE)

4.) **WARM-DOWN**: 10 MIN.

GYMNASTIC DRESSAGE

DAY 1: DRESSAGE

DAY 2: GYMNASTIC JUMPING

DAY 3: DAY OFF

DAY 4: DRESSAGE

DAY 5: COURSE JUMPING

DAY 6: 2 HOURS OUT ON TRAILS

DAY 7: DRESSAGE

The novice level introduces track work. It is very important to understand the purpose of this conditioning level. Until now the horse has been working at a slow, muscle-building regimen. In this level we will be using a more formal version of training called LSD (long slow distance) work. This phase is very important in helping to strengthen the horse's tendons and ligaments, which helps to prevent injury later when we start gallops and more demanding fences. Until now we have been developing the horse's respiratory, circulatory and muscular systems, but the structural systems of the horse take longer to develop and are the most important for preventing injuries. The track work is an aerobic workout. It is at this phase where you should use a heart rate monitor during workouts, to alert you to any difficulties the horse may have internally which he is failing to communicate to you. You don't have to own a heart rate monitor; you can monitor heart rates without one. Average heart rates are as follows: standing 25-60, walking 50-90, trotting 80-130, cantering 120-160. These rates will vary between horses, therefore it is important to monitor and track the progress of your horse's heart rates.

The phrase "track work" is used in the rest of this book. This phrase is defined here as "the track work beginning your workout, a warm-up of LSD work, and not to be confused with galloping on a track." The "track work" is carried out in a large area, not necessarily on a track. Having access to a track is certainly a plus, but a large field with good footing or the wide stretch along a road will work as well. Get the horse out in the open, not working in circles. If you have a track or access to one, it should be at least a half-mile long. **The most important point is to find good footing, while not requiring circling of the horse.** Your gallops, which will come later, will also need good footing and long stretches in a large area. Dressage work will include enough circling of the horse and get him out of the arena into a large area with good footing. Continuous circling during a workout is very hard on a horse's ligaments and joints!

This track-work period will be carried out before each workout for the rest of the horse's schedule, with the exception of the two-hour walk days. Each workout should begin with warming up over cavelletti, which can be conveniently placed next to the track. Then proceed to a half-mile walk with the horse in a long and low position. Not a deep and low position of the neck, but one where the horse has his nose stretched down towards the ground. In my opinion it is never a good idea to overbend the neck into the horse's chest! Another half mile at a trot in the same position, followed by a canter in a long and low frame. Keeping the horse moving forward from behind in a long and low frame will build his back muscles. Then change directions and start all over again. The horse is not to be working on speed at this point, keep him at medium speeds throughout each gait.

It is recommended to use a half-mile track, any track of less distance is dangerous for the horse's legs with the gallops which will come later. The track could be sand or grass, but it needs to be flat, without ruts, and soft, but not at all deep. This area could be managed by using a plugging aerator to reduce concussion in the horse's legs.

Following the track work you should spend approximately ten minutes warming up with dressage basics, which you practiced in the initial levels. Use a combination of stretches, bending exercises, lateral movements, collection and extension exercises, etc. Try to vary it a little, but this is just a stretching and warm-up phase, so keep it simple. Your next step will depend on your scheduled day. Either you will stay in the dressage ring or you will move on to jumping. If you stay in the dressage ring, work on the exercises you taught the horse in the first four levels. Don't dismiss the trail walking days. They are important for the horse's mind and body. They help the horse to build endurance slowly while not placing stress on his legs.

If you are scheduled for gymnastic jumping, remember to warm-up over smaller jumps first. By the end of this level your mount should be comfortable practicing gymnastic jumps as high as **two feet three inches**; increase gradually. You are also introducing course jumping at this phase, alternate the course jumping days between the stadium course and the cross-country course. You should be working at Novice levels and, therefore, at Novice speeds. In the novice level on the cross-country course you often have time to canter the course and trot the fences. This helps the horse get used to steadying and collecting before each fence on the cross-country field. At this level **do not exceed any jumping over three-feet three inches**. The purpose is to keep the rider from jumping the horse higher than necessary and before the horse is ready. Save your horse's legs. Unless you are also showing the horse as a jumper, there is no need to increase the height of the fences at this Novice level just for your own thrills! You will be responsible for knowing the requirements at each level of competition. Know the dressage tests, the jump heights and widths, speeds, etc. that you will be asked to perform at horse trials. How your horse performs at the competitions will allow you to determine when it is time to move on to the next level from here on out!

# SAMPLE GYMNASTIC EXERCISES

# FOR NOVICE LEVEL

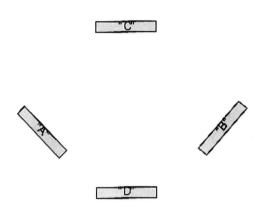

Set up four cavalletti per diagram, with plenty of space
between them to trot and canter from any one of them
to another. Practice turning and jumping from both
leads equally. Keep yourself and the horse balanced
and calm. Be careful not to drill the horse. Give him
breaks often, letting him walk with dropped reins.

# I I I I X H 1

Set this line up with your oxer after the cross rail and a
vertical after the oxer. Give the horse 19 feet after the
cross rail and 21 feet between the oxer and the vertical.
These distances are approximate, be sure the horse is
comfortable with the distances you choose. Your
jumps should be 2 feet 3 inches at this level.

# I I I I X H H

Keep this line the same as the last, but change the
vertical to an oxer and set 30 feet between the two
oxers. Your oxers can be two feet wide now.

# TRAINING LEVEL

\* EACH DAY WILL BEGIN WITH TRACK WORK
AND WARM UP FROM THE NOVICE LEVEL.

**DAY 1**: 20 MIN. STRONG TROT & 15 MIN.
GYMNASTIC JUMPING

**DAY 2**: DRESSAGE

**DAY 3**: 2 x 1-MILE GALLOPS W/ 7 MIN.
TROT/WLK B/T EACH MILE

**DAY 4**: 2 HOUR WALK ON TRAILS (no track work,
only suppling)

**DAY 5**: DRESSAGE

**DAY 6**: COURSE JUMPING

**DAY 7**: DAY OFF

The Training level introduces two gallops into the workouts. The average heart rate at a gallop is 150-200 beats/min. These gallops should be kept slower, under control, not exceeding 500 meters/minute. The rest period after the gallops should be 5 minutes of trotting, followed by 2min. walking. The time spent trotting should start as a strong trot, then taper to a slow medium trot. While walking you should incorporate suppling and stretching exercises in the last few minutes (leg-yielding, half-halts, bending, long and low stretches, etc.). The trotting is meant to rid the muscles of lactic acid, and the long walk is imperative in allowing oxygen to reach deep tissues in order to prevent injury. These gallops are anaerobic exercises while the LSD work was an aerobic exercise. During anaerobic exercise the tissues are basically operating under oxygen deprived conditions and need time to recover between bouts of exercise. This is a type of interval training; the rest period is of utmost importance. In studying the oxygen deprivation of deep tissues within the legs and joints it has been found that this extra time is needed to allow oxygen levels to recover. Some people think this rest period should be only a few minutes. Allow the horse every chance to prevent injury! It should go without saying that during the gallops, you will shorten your stirrups and stay off the horse's back at all times, just like on the cross-country course. Working on the track as an exercise rider is an excellent training for these gallops and the cross-country phase in general. I encourage all my students to get a job at a track at an early point in their career. It is useful in teaching many techniques in handling horses in many different circumstances. Your first gallop of the day should always be carried out at the slowest speed. The gallop should start out slower and increase to your maximum speed gradually. Your fastest speed could peak in the middle of your gallops or toward the end. You can adjust your speed within the gallops to peak and then slow again at the end. The point is that you may have a goal of 500m/minutes, but you will start your first quarter mile at 450, then the next quarter mile at 475, the next quarter at 500, then the last quarter at 475 again. You will have to use your own judgment or get a trainer's opinion to do what works best for your horse. The type, length and speed of your gallops will depend on the horse's breed, fitness, and temperament. This is part of the schedule you may have to customize the most. Use a stopwatch and marked distances to know your speeds during your gallops. Learn how to judge the speed of the gallops by feel.

At this level, the gymnastic jumping should be raised to **two feet and six inches**; the course jumping in this level should gradually reach, but **not exceed, a height of four-feet** fences. It goes without saying these fences should be inviting and straight forward. This is a good time to introduce the horse to lead changes as well. Use common sense; if you have an event coming up, take it easy for a few days before to allow the horse any healing and time to rest up for the event. Do not jump heavily or gallop seven to ten days before the event. Do only cavalletti work, track work (the long and low warm-up) and dressage. A light day of gymnastic jumping may be necessary for some horses a few days prior to an event. Two days off, assuming the horse is without injury or stress, is appropriate following a competition at this level. The first day back into work usually starts with the walk on trails, then resume the schedule from there. If the event is merely a few dressage classes at a dressage show, one day off is sufficient. During the year at the Training level it is a good idea to go to many clinics, dressage shows, and hunter/jumper shows to increase the horse's experiences and skills. One combined training event per month, with one of the other shows or clinics in between, is a good schedule. The horses will become sour if they are hauled somewhere every weekend, therefore try to give them an every other weekend schedule. This is a good time to introduce the horse to bounces (no stride between jumps) in his gymnastic exercises, as well as practicing skinnies (5 to 6 feet narrow jumps) in your course work.

When preparing for an event, count backwards from the date of the event to set up your schedule. The key is to have the horse in his peak of conditioning at the time of the event. **You must customize your schedule for the horse you are riding; they will all need varying programs.**

# SAMPLE GYMNASTIC EXERCISES FOR

## TRAINING LEVEL

# I I I X 1 1 1

Set up this exercise with 12 feet after the cross rail and 20 feet between the verticals. Your jumps should be 2 feet 6 inches at this level.

# I I I X 1 1 H

Set up this exercise with 10 feet 6 inches after the cross rail and change the last vertical to an oxer. Your oxers can be 2 foot 3 inches wide now.

# I I I I X 1 H 1

Change the second vertical to an oxer and set the last
jump up as a vertical. You will have to give the horse
more distance between the oxer and the last vertical.
An oxer increases the distance needed between fences
because the horse covers more ground upon landing
from an oxer. Increase the distance following the oxer
between 25 to 28 feet, depending on your horse's
stride.

# PRELIMINARY LEVEL

\* EACH DAY WILL BEGIN WITH TRACK
WORK AND WARM-UP
FROM THE NOVICE LEVEL.

**DAY 1**: 3 x 1 MILE GALLOPS W/ 7 MIN.
TRT/WLK B/T EACH MILE

**DAY 2**: 2 HOUR WALK ON TRAILS (no
track work, only suppling)

**DAY 3**: DRESSAGE

**DAY 4**: COURSE JUMPING

**DAY 5**: DRESSAGE & 1 MILE GALLOP

**DAY 6**: 30 MIN. STRONG TROT &
GYMNASTIC JUMPING

**DAY 7**: DAY OFF

At this point the horse should be a confident, bold jumper, as well as performing proficiently in dressage. Don't push goals for dressage for each stage, because each horse must work at his own pace. Dressage lessons every two weeks with a dressage instructor who is aware of the combined training tests and goals is very important, as well as dressage clinics and dressage shows, where much can be learned about areas that may need further honing. Much can be learned by auditing clinics. Auditing a clinic is cheaper than taking your horse and you get to watch every lesson. Take your horse when you can and audit others!

The gymnastic jumps could be moved up to a height of **two feet nine inches.** Lead changes should be mastered at this point in the horse's career. The cross-country work should be more challenging at this level, including water jumps, drops, combinations, banks, etc. Stadium fences could increase to, but shouldn't exceed, a **final height of four feet three inches** and the gallops could gradually increase to a speed of 525m/minutes. Notice the rest time between gallops increases as well; this is important for tissue recovery and injury prevention. Again, you will have to customize the speeds and distances to your individual horse. Remember that speed is what breaks down horse's legs; it is better to increase distance at a slower speed.

The preliminary level can be a deciding factor as to how far your horse may advance. If you have a horse that is very successful at this level, you may have a horse that could compete through the advanced level of competition. At this level, it is important to school many cross-country courses, acquainting the horse with many obstacles. I also cannot emphasize enough the importance of time spent on leg care. Your time will pay off! At this level the horse will be introduced to greater physical stresses than he has yet encountered.

The thirty-minute strong trot at this phase is to help increase endurance and strength without adding the concussion to the legs with more gallops. The strong trot is meant to be at least 300 m/min. Use hills if you have them available to you. The strong trot should be followed by a walking period of ten minutes with suppling exercises before moving on to the gymnastic jumping.

If your horse is going well in the preliminary horse trials and getting through the jumping phases without incurring jumping or time penalties; you could try to enter one three-day preliminary event (CCI*) before the end of this season. This event will give you a good idea of how far your horse can go through the levels and how he can handle himself with the extra endurance factor. A late fall event would be good timing. He should be able to compete in a Preliminary three-day after having the whole season to train and prepare. You will have to change his schedule to increase his endurance abilities. Longer strong trots and more hill work could be used. You will have to adapt the horse to the steeplechase phase, and your timing will be even more important for you to learn. Be sure to set up a schedule working backwards from the three-day event, peaking at the time of the event. You will need much guidance to prepare for a three-day, and I will leave this topic for another book.

# I I I I X H 1 H

Set this line up with an oxer following the cross rails, then a vertical, then an oxer. Your oxers can be 2 foot 6 inches wide now.   Your jumps should be 2 feet 9 inches at this level.

# I I I I X 1 H  H

This line will change your last three fences to a vertical followed by two oxers.  You will need lots of impulsion coming through the line for the horse to stretch over an oxer, take a stride and stretch over another oxer.  Again, give the horse 30 feet between oxers.

# I I I I X X H 1 1

This exercise requires a bounce between the cross rails, one stride to the oxer, two strides to a vertical and one stride to the last vertical.

# INTERMEDIATE & ADVANCED

\* EACH DAY WILL BEGIN WITH TRACK WORK AND WARM-UP FROM THE NOVICE LEVEL.

**DAY 1**: 4 x 1 MILE GALLOPS W/ 10 MIN. TRT/WLK B/T EACH MILE

**DAY 2**: 2 HOUR WALK ON TRAILS (no track work, only suppling)

**DAY 3**: 30 MIN. STRONG TROT & GYMNASTIC JUMPING

**DAY 4**: DRESSAGE

**DAY 5**: DAY OFF

**DAY 6**: 4 x 1 MILE GALLOPS W/ 10 MIN. TRT/WLK B/T EACH MILE

**DAY 7**: 2 HOUR WALK ON TRAILS (no track work, only suppling)

**DAY 8**: COURSE JUMPING

**DAY 9**: DRESSAGE

**DAY 10**: DAY OFF

I  I  I  I  X  1   H

Set this line up with two strides after the cross rail and
three strides between the vertical and the oxer.  Your
oxers can be up to three feet wide now.  Your jumps
should be 3 feet for intermediate and 3 feet 3 inches for
advanced.

I  I  I  I  X  H  H  1

Set this line up with two strides after the cross rail and
between the oxers, then one stride between the oxer
and the vertical.

# I I I I X I I X I I I H

This line introduces cavalletti between jumps. Set a cavalletti 10 feet after the cross rail, then 10 feet after that one, then ten feet to another cross rail. Follow that with ten feet between the next three cavalletti and to an oxer.

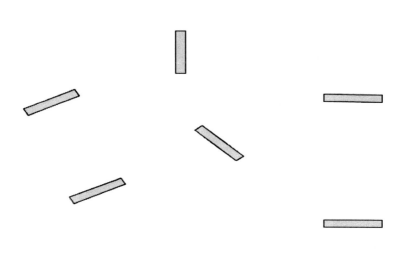

IIIII X X H

Set up a course of jumps like the one shown here, with your gymnastic line along the side of the ring. You can then change your gymnastic line as you need to and it will always be available on your gymnastic jumping days. A course set with jumps at different angles will allow you to change the direction and route quite often. You will need to change a few jumps around and make different combinations often to pose different questions to the horse.

The last level is for both the Intermediate and the Advanced levels of horse trials, not three-day events. The Advanced level is more demanding in athletic ability than the Intermediate level. Depending on the type of event, it is usually more challenging in every phase. You will notice that the week has suddenly become longer and the schedule more complicated. By the time you have reached this level you will know your horse well and will know what works best for him. At these levels the conditioning schedules will tend to vary the most as different horses need different schedules and you prepare the horse for different events. Your horse must be in the proper condition for the event you are preparing for at a certain point in time. He must peak at the time of the competition and not be over or under fit for the job. This is a point where you must rely more on a trainer and vet to help you decide what your horse needs. Does he need more hill work? More gallop work? More trot work? More experience with gymnastic jumping? More work in the dressage arena? These are all questions that you must ask yourself and a professional to determine how to further develop your horse's athletic ability and fitness level for the competition scheduled.

The gallops scheduled are only guidelines. Use one gallop day in the schedule to work on shorter, faster gallops. The second gallop day can then be used to work on longer, slower gallops. The speed of your gallops may increase as you advance in competition. Remember that it is the increased speed of your gallops that will break the horse's legs down. This is a point in the horse's career which you must become much more technical about training him and taking care of his legs. A microscopic tear in a tendon or ligament following a gallop could go unnoticed and turn into a major problem following your next jumping day. Be sure you warm-up and cool-down properly. Do not maintain a schedule if the horse doesn't feel right. If he doesn't seem to be his "ready to work self," then something is bothering him, and he deserves some time off to determine what that may be, even if he isn't lame. By the time you reach these levels you will know that horse well and know when he isn't himself; don't ignore his cues! His heart rate can also be an indicator of hidden pain in his body. It may increase before any lameness show up in the horse.

For the Intermediate level, the gallops could increase to 550 m/min. and the gymnastic jumps should increase to **three feet.** The course jumping should **not exceed four feet six inches** and cross-country courses will be much more challenging. By this level, give the horse at least five days off following an event. The horse will experience more demanding problems on his cross-country courses and will need to strengthen this area the most.

For the Advanced level, the gallops can increase to 575 m/min. and the gymnastics increase to **three feet three inches**. The course jumping should **not exceed four feet nine inches,** and I would give at least six days off following an event.

If this program has worked as planned, you could have a horse that may be nine or ten years old and has reached the advanced level in eventing while remaining sound throughout his career. Of course, this is not a perfect world, and many horses will repeat seasons due to either lameness or lack of confidence, maybe even lack of skill. Some horses will not be athletic enough to pass certain levels. The important thing to remember is to **find what works for your horse and customize his schedule to benefit his training and conditioning.**

I have not discussed the different levels of events, trials, etc.; you will need a good instructor to teach you these things as you go through the levels. The previous schedule is meant to prepare a horse for horse trials. Three-day events are very different and much more demanding. You may want to graduate to these levels as you gain more knowledge. A regular schedule of lessons, one per week while alternating the dressage and jumping lessons, is the one way to learn fast enough to keep up with this schedule, until you have moved through the Advanced level. I advise a rotation of cross-country jumping and stadium jumping with your lessons as well. Keep an open mind and learn as much as you can from as many trainers, vets, riders, professors, etc. Attend as many clinics as possible.  Volunteering with you local Eventing organization can be a great way to learn more about the sport.  Being a cross-country jump judge at different events is both educational and rewarding!  Read books and magazines, watch videos, etc. to gain knowledge from every area in the equine world!!

    – My best wishes and good luck!!!


Elizabeth Grisell-Short

# HEART RATES ON FLAT GROUND

| ACTIVITY | SPEED | HEART RATE |
|----------|-------|------------|
| Standing | 0 m/min | 25-60 beats/min. |
| Walking | 125 | 50-90 |
| Trotting | 250-300 | 80-150 |
| Cantering | 350 | 120-160 |
| Galloping | 500 | 150-200 |

Practice checking your horse's heart rate on the front of the left jawbone, on the large artery, with your fingers (do not use your thumb). Checking your horse's heart rate is an important indicator of his fitness level. The table above includes averages for heart rates at differing efforts. The important aspect of tracking a horse's heart rate is not just what the rate is at different paces, but what your specific horse's rate is at that pace on that day. You may want to keep a chart of your horse's rates at varied times during his workout. Another important factor to track is his recovery rates. As the horse becomes more fit he will not only have a lower heart rate during a certain effort, he will also have lower rates through his recovery time. For example, check his rate immediately following a gallop and again after 30 seconds and one minute of walking (or trotting). The rate can then be checked after one more minute and so on until his rate is back to average for his current effort. Over time you can plot a graph which will indicate his rates declining as he becomes more fit. Heart rate is an indicator of many functions going on in the horse's body. It will increase if he is hurting, or scared, or mad, etc. His emotions will need to be noted as well if they seem to be affecting his normal rates. A horse's heart rate may be elevated if he is dealing with pain even if he is not showing that pain to you in any other way. Therefore, heart rate monitoring can be used as a tool to detect lameness before it shows up in their gaits. If you can't determine the reason for your horse's increased heart rate, have his blood chemistry checked with a CBP. You may find he is fighting an infection or his electrolytes are out of balance.

An adult horse should have a resting heart rate between 30 – 40 beats per minute. A rate of 50 bpm indicates stress, 60 bpm is definitely abnormal, and 80 is an emergency. Horses have recorded a rate of greater than 200 bpm in intense exercise, but a well-conditioned horse is more likely to have a heart rate of 100 bpm in intense exercise and drop to less than 70 bpm within 30 minutes. A horse doing interval training or gallops, should be allowed to return to 70 bpm before another bout of exercise. This will decrease risk of injury caused by oxygen deprivation to the tissues.

# **DAILY EQUINE REPORT CARD**

AM CHECK:
       FEET

       LEGS

       TEMPERATURE

       HEART RATE

       COMMENTS:


PM CHECK:
       FEET

       LEGS

       TEMPURATURE

       HEART RATE

       COMMENTS:


WORKOUT CONDITIONS:


TYPE OF WORKOUT:

MAX. HEART RATE DURING WORKOUT:


AREAS OF DIFFICULTY:




ADDITIONAL COMMENTS:

# EVENT & TRAVEL

# SUPPLIES

- EXTRA HALTERS
- EXTRA LEADS
- TRAILER JACK
- TIRE GAUGE & FIX-A-FLAT
- FLARES & FLASH LIGHTS
- SHIPPING BOOTS
- GROOMING BOX
- FLY SPRAY
- EQUINE FIRST AID
- BATHING KIT
- BRAIDING KIT
- TOWELS
- HARDWARE & TOOL KIT
- HAY NETS
- HOOF CARE KIT
- ROPE
- FAN
- EXTENSION CORD
- WATER HEATER
- HOSE

- MANURE BUCKET & PITCH FORK
- STUD KIT
- DUCT TAPE
- SCISSORS
- TACK CLEANING KIT
- BOOT POLISHING KIT
- MEDICINE KIT
- HUMAN FIRST AID KIT
- HEART RATE MONITOR
- TWITCH
- LUNGE LINE
- SHEETS & COOLERS & BLANKETS
- CLIPPERS
- CROSS TIES
- LEATHER PUNCH
- STALL GUARDS
- STALL INFO CARDS
- WATER BUCKETS
- FEED BUCKETS
- STALL TOYS
- EASY BOOTS
- CHAIRS
- ICE COOLER
- FOOD & DRINKS

- EXTRA COATS
- EXTRA BOOTS
- RAIN GEAR
- CHAPS
- BELL BOOTS
- GALLOPING BOOTS
- STANDING WRAPS
- POULTICE
- X-COUNTRY GREASE
- VET WRAP
- X-COUNTRY SADDLE & GIRTH
- X-COUNTRY SADDLE PADS
- X-COUNTRY BRIDLE & MARTINGALES
- OVER GIRTH & BREASTPLATE
- X-COUNTRY WATCH
- X-COUNTRY VEST
- X-COUNTRY HELMET
- X-COUNTRY WATCH
- X-COUNTRY BELT
- X-COUNTRY BOOTS
- X-COUNTRY BREECHES
- X-COUNTRY SHIRT
- X-COUNTRY GLOVES
- X-COUNTRY BAT

- MEDICAL ARM BAND
- STADIUM SADDLE PADS
- STADIUM SADDLE & GIRTH
- STADIUM BRIDLE & MARTINGALES
- STADIUM HORSE BOOTS
- STADIUM BREASTPLATE
- STADIUM BAT
- STADIUM SPURS
- STADIUM COAT & SHIRTS
- STADIUM BREECHES
- STADIUM HELMET
- STADIUM GLOVES
- EXTRA BITS
- DRESSAGE SADDLE PADS
- DRESSAGE SADDLE & GIRTH
- DRESSAGE BRIDLE
- DRESSAGE HAT
- DRESSAGE COAT & SHIRTS
- DRESSAGE BREECHES
- DRESSAGE BOOTS
- DRESSAGE GLOVES
- DRESSAGE TIES & PINS
- DRESSAGE SPURS
- USEF RULE BOOK

- USEA OMNIBUS
- MAPS & DIRECTIONS
- COGGINS & HEALTH CERTIFICATE
- INSURANCE INFO.
- FEED & SUPPLEMENTS
- BEDDING & HAY
- HORSE TREATS
- OTHER:
- OTHER:
- OTHER:
- OTHER:
- OTHER:
- OTHER:
- 
-

# BETH'S HERBAL APPLESAUCE HORSE COOKIES

2 Tablespoons (30ml) Seasalt

2 Tablespoons (30ml) Garlic Powder

2 cups (424ml) Mint, Oregano, & Rosemary
(Fresh and minced)*

1 cup (237ml) Applesauce

1 ½ cups (355ml) Wholewheat Flour

2 cups (355ml) Quick Oats

1 cup (237ml) Molasses

½ cup (118ml) Brown Sugar

1 cup (237ml) Flaxseed


Spray cooking sheets with cooking oil. Drop batter
onto sheets, one tablespoon at a time and flatten on top.
Cook one hour at 200F. Flip treats over and cook
another hour.

*If using dried herbs, add ½ cup of water to batter.

# BOOKS AND VIDEOS

**GENERAL:**

LUNGING THE HORSE & RIDER – Sheila Inderwick

CAVALLETTI – Reiner Klimke

TRAINING THE EVENT HORSE AND RIDER – James Wofford

PRACTICAL EVENTING – Sally O'Conner

THE STARTING BOX – Barbara Ernest

USEA RULE BOOK

HORSES ARE MADE TO BE HORSES – Franz Mairinger

CENTERED RIDING – Sally Swift

**DRESSAGE:**

COMMON SENSE DRESSAGE – Sally O'Connor

(VIDEO DRESSAGE SERIES) – Kyra Kyrklund

(VIDEO DREASSAGE SERIES) – Reiner Klimke


**JUMPING:**

HUNTER SEAT EQUITATION – George Morris

RIDING AND JUMPING – William Steinkraus

CLASSIC SHOW JUMPING – Bertalan de Nemethy

**CROSS-COUNTRY:**

NOVICE COURSE WALK with DAVID O'CONNOR (video)

CROSS-COUNTRY RIDING – Lucinda Green

CROSS-COUNTRY CLINIC – Blyth Tait

THE STUD BOOK – Malcolm E. Kelly


**NUTRITION:**

PREVENTING COLIC IN HORSES – Dr. Christine King

FEEDING TO WIN II – Equine Research, Inc.

HORSE NUTRITION – Harold F. Hintz, Ph.D.

EQUINE SUPPLEMENTS & NUTRACEUTICALS – Eleanor M. Kellon, VMD


**CONDITIONING:**

CONDITIONING TO WIN – Equine Research, Inc.

CONDITIONING SPORT HORSES – Hilary M. Clayton

IF YOU CAN'T FIND ANY OF THESE BOOKS OR VIDEOS, FIND A SIMILAR ONE. The list above was chosen from my personal library. There are many, well-written books on the market; these are just a few to help you find some on different topics. Since you have chosen the sport of Eventing, you must gain a wide variety of knowledge! Some tack stores rent out videos as well as books. Other books and videos can be purchased, but can be used over and over as a reference during your training.

# Bibliography

Allen, Linda L. and Dianna R. Dennis. *101 Jumping Exercises for Horse & Rider.* North Adams, MA: Storey Publishing.


Clayton, Hilary M. *Conditioning Sport Horses.* Saskatoon, Saskatchewan: Sport Horse Publications, 1991.


Equine Research. *Feeding to Win.* Tyler, Texas: Equine Research Publications, 1973


Equine Research. *Veterinary Treatments & Medications for Horsemen.* Tyler, Texas: Equine Research Publications, 1977

Garlinghouse, Susan and Barney Flemming. *How To Read a Blood Panel in One Easy Lesson.* Pride Project Info Equine Health Resources, www.equinedoc.com.

Hintz, Harold F. *Horse Nutrition, A Practical Guide.* New York, NY: Arco Publishing, 1983

Kellon, Eleanor M. *Equine Supplements & Nutraceuticals, A Guide To Peak Health and Performance.* Ossining, NY: Breakthrough Publishing, 1998.

King, Christene. *Preventing Colic in Horses.* Cary, NC: Paper Horse, 1999.

King, Christene and Mansmann, Richard. *Equine Lameness*. Tyler, Texas: Equine Research, Inc., 1997.

Klimke, Ingrid & Reiner. *Cavelletti, The Schooling of Horse and Rider Over Ground Poles.* Guilford, Connectiut: The Lyons Press, 1985

Mansmann, Richard and Christine King. *Preventing Laminitis In Horses.* Cary, NC: Paper Horse, 2000.

Ross, Mike W. and Sue J. Dyson. *Diagnosis and Management of Lameness In The Horse.* St. Louis, Missouri: Elsevier Science, 2003

Elizabeth Short grew up showing hunters and jumpers on the competitive "A" circuits. While living on a horse farm raising and training sport horses for showing and fox hunting, she learned the importance of proper management and conditioning. By the age of twelve she was breaking horses raised on the family's farm. She started breaking horses for other people by the time she was thirteen. She gained a great deal of experience training horses and competing on a national level. Showing hunters on the "A" circuit gave her the great asset of attaining an equitation based seat. By the age of sixteen she began breaking and training horses as a profession. Two years later she was gaining the experience of working thoroughbreds on the track. Over the next few years she trained horses, taught at camps and studied dressage. During this time Elizabeth studied nutrition at Purdue University. She spent time training horses in Australia for the racetrack, and retraining horses off the track for the sport of Combined Training (Eventing). Upon returning to the United States she began competing her own horse in Combined Training and acquired many students in the sport. She had learned a great deal about conditioning horses on the tracks. Her knowledge of dressage, jumping, conditioning and nutrition came together in training for this sport. She was surprised to see so many horses unfit at competitions, especially up through the Preliminary level. Many of her students did not know how to condition their horses on a daily basis to prepare them for the differing levels of this challenging sport. Other students needed help with horses due to improper conditioning, causing soreness through their body and legs. Elizabeth saw a need for the knowledge of proper conditioning and management techniques in this sport. She wrote this book as a guide for her students and other serious equestrians who want to compete in the sport of Eventing, while keeping their horses fit and sound.

Elizabeth Grisell-Short now raises, trains, and competes sport horses at Fox Fire Farms. Fox Fire Farms is an Event training facility in North Carolina. The farm is complete with a stadium jumping ring, regulation dressage ring, cross-country course, half-mile track and indoor arena. For more information visit the website at *www.mysporthorse.com*.

CPSIA information can be obtained at www.ICGtesting.com
Printed in the USA
BVOW03s0410020813

327446BV00003B/423/P